GLASGOW

THE CLASSIC THEN AND NOW PHOTOGRAPHS

JAMES McCARROLL

Contemporary photographs by Duncan I. McEwan

Fort Publishing Ltd

Contents

Front cover | *George Square, from the south-west, 1904*

Glasgow's fine civic square dates from the 1780s and was originally composed of elegant Georgian terraces, residences of the great and the good. Gradually, however, it was subsumed by commerce and municipal administration, and, in particular, that symbol of Glasgow: the city chambers. The building was designed by Paisley man William Young, who won a rigorous competition for the brief, and completed in 1888, when Queen Victoria performed the opening ceremony. Young's aim was to bring the Italian Renaissance, and more specifically Venice, to Glasgow and the magnificent façade splendidly succeeds in that aim. The interior, if anything, is even more impressive, especially the marble staircases.

Back cover | *George Square, from the south-west, 2012*

Apart from the city chambers there is much of interest in the square, most notably the Scott Monument (*centre*) of 1837, which was erected five years after the death of the eponymous Sir Walter Scott. Despite the great novelist's Edinburgh connections it was the first such commemoration of him anywhere. There are many other fine statues in George Square, including those honouring Queen Victoria and Prince Albert, Sir Robert Peel, Robert Burns and James Watt.

Preface

Many of the old photographs here date from the late-Victorian and Edwardian eras. That is hardly surprising. In this period, Glasgow was transformed into arguably the greatest industrial city in the world. The word 'Clydebuilt' became synonymous with quality as its shipyards and factories led the world in productivity and innovation. In these years, it was calculated that Glasgow produced upwards of one-fifth of the world's ships.

As great fortunes were made, the men behind them built lavish mansions and wonderful public buildings to advertise their wealth. The sheer scale of the new architecture was to make Glasgow, in the eyes of many, the most impressive Victorian city on earth. Great architects such as Alexander 'Greek' Thomson, John Honeyman, Charles Wilson, Sir George Gilbert Scott and, of course, Charles Rennie Mackintosh gave Glasgow an architectural heritage second to none. Glasgow's civic pride was eloquently expressed by the opulence of the city chambers in George Square while, in the west of the city, elegant terraces were laid out to accommodate a burgeoning and self-confident middle class.

Glasgow, however, also had an important history prior to the Industrial Revolution. By the twelfth century it had not only the beginnings of what was to become an impressive cathedral but also a bishop's castle and associated ecclesiastical properties. By the fifteenth century it boasted a university and, in 1611, the 'dear green place' was raised to the status of a royal burgh by King James VI. Then, in the first great wave of commercialisation, along came the Tobacco Lords, many of whom built fine houses to the west of Glasgow Cross.

Sadly, but perhaps inevitably, much of old Glasgow has been swept away. There were many factors: slum clearance, the coming of the railways, fire, the M8 motorway. This book reflects that change. Some of the old photos collected here are all we have left of important city landmarks like the Old College buildings of Glasgow University, Anderston Cross, St Enoch Station and Kelvinside House.

It is fortunate that much of value has been preserved, especially from the Victorian period. Delights like the Western Club in Buchanan Street, the Ca' d'Oro in Union Street and Charing Cross Mansions are essential stops for anyone interested in Victorian architecture and the history of this great city.

I will mention three personal favourites. The Stewart Memorial Fountain in Kelvingrove Park, with its delightful carvings and statuary, as well as its fully functioning water jets, would probably be on most people's list, as would St Andrew's church, a serendipitous pleasure in the sometimes overlooked Saltmarket area. A lesser known gem is the Cameronian war memorial (page 83), a wonderfully vivid evocation of men in battle and a fitting tribute to them.

We are fortunate that Glasgow attracted many innovative photographers during the Victorian and Edwardian eras: men like Francis Frith and George Washington Wilson, who chronicled towns and cities the length and breadth of Britain. Their work is well represented in these pages. The city, however, had its own men of vision, most notably Thomas Annan. Born in Fife, Annan came to Glasgow as a young man to work for Joseph Swan, a well-known engraver and lithographer. Before long Annan struck out on his own, establishing a photographic business in Woodlands Road and then moving to more fashionable premises in Sauchiehall Street, from where he captured Victorian Glasgow for posterity. He was a technical and artistic giant, one of the true pioneers of photography, and after his death in 1887 the mantle was taken up by his son, James Craig Annan, a considerable artist in his own right. Both men feature prominently in these pages.

The photographs have been ordered, if somewhat loosely, on a geographical basis. Beginning in Townhead we proceed down High Street to the Glasgow Cross area, and then move west along Trongate to the city centre. This is followed by sections on the west end, the river Clyde and its environs and, finally, the south side.

James McCarroll, July 2012

Title page | *Argyle Street, looking west 1888 and 2012*

Then, as now, Argyle Street was one of the city's busiest shopping thoroughfares. On the right is Miller Street, while Dunlop Street, once home to the Union Hotel, is on the left. The flagstaffs of John Anderson's famous Victorian department store, the Royal Polytechnic, are visible on the left of the 1888 photograph. Like its near neighbour, Buchanan Street, Argyle Street has also been pedestrianised, as the 2012 image illustrates. Anderson's Royal Polytechnic was demolished in 1933 and replaced by Lewis's, a department store on seven storeys in Portland stone with some neat Art Deco touches, which later morphed into a branch of Debenham's.

◄ *Glasgow Cathedral from the Necropolis, 1900*
There has been a Christian presence on this site – the hillside of the Molendinar Burn – since the time of Glasgow's first bishop, Kentigern (St Mungo), in the sixth century. However, the construction of the cathedral we see today probably dates from the late twelfth century. According to one leading architectural historian the cathedral is 'the most important building of its period surviving in Scotland'. The interior is delightful, with the choir, crypt and the Blackadder aisle (named after Archbishop Blackadder) especially noteworthy.

▲ *Glasgow Cathedral from the Necropolis, 2012*
The building to the left, and right, of the cathedral is Glasgow Royal Infirmary, which was an early twentieth century replacement for Robert Adam's original infirmary of 1792. Many opposed James Miller's design for the new infirmary, arguing that it would over-whelm the medieval cathedral. The Bridge of Sighs, gateway to Glasgow's spectacular necropolis, is in the foreground.

THE OLDEST HOUSE IN GLASGOW. BRANDON SER

▲ *Provand's Lordship, Castle Street, 1904*

Built in 1471 by Bishop Andrew Muirhead as part of the adjoining St Nicholas's hospital (now lost), Provand's Lordship is said to be the oldest surviving house in Glasgow. Apart from the cathedral, it is the only remaining structure from the ecclesiastical enclave that occupied this part of Townhead in medieval times. The word Provand derives from 'prebend', which relates to a stipend paid by a cathedral to clergy. At the time this photograph was taken the house was being used for commercial purposes, including a sweet shop and advertising hoarding.

▶ *Provand's Lordship, Castle Street, 2012*

The building was saved from the wave of redevelopment that swept through Glasgow in the late nineteenth century thanks to the efforts of the Provand's Lordship Society, which restored it to former glories in 1906. Today Provand's Lordship is a museum with a fine collection of seventeenth century furniture, some of it donated by shipping magnate Sir William Burrell, a noted collector and patron of the arts. The tenements that surrounded it have been demolished.

High Street, looking south to Glasgow Cross, early 1870s
Originally the link between Glasgow Cathedral and Glasgow Cross, High Street has been the subject of several waves of redevelopment. Much of this was due to the arrival of the railways, which of course displaced the former Glasgow University buildings when that institution moved to the west of the city in the 1870s. By the time this photograph was taken High Street was one of the poorer parts of the city, full of brothels, shebeens (unlicensed pubs) and pawnbrokers (*left*).

High Street, looking south to Glasgow Cross, 2012
Remaining buildings of quality were swept away in the twentieth century. Particularly grievous was the loss in 1973
of two neo-classical tenement blocks by James Adam, which stood at the entrance to College Street (*right*).

Old College, University of Glasgow, High Street 1870 and Old College site, High Street 2012

The building style of the Old College is Scottish Renaissance and the main entrance, where the cab is parked, was heavily ornamented with a coat of arms above. Considered by many good judges to be the finest seventeenth century building in Scotland, the Old College's fate was sealed when the site was sold to a railway company in the 1860s. A few years later the University of Glasgow decamped to a new campus at Gilmorehill, in the infinitely more fashionable and salubrious west end of the city. Today, the architecture on this section of High Street is considerably less distinguished.

11

Glasgow Cross, 1914

Glasgow Cross, 2012

The Tolbooth Steeple of 1814 (*centre, both photographs*) by David Hamilton is the only remnant of Glasgow's original municipal buildings since the main part was demolished in 1921 to make way for a reorganisation of the streets around Glasgow Cross. That 1814 building was itself a replacement for the original tollbooth, which dates from the seventeenth century and functioned as Glasgow's town hall, court and prison. As one observer notes, the Steeple has a 'splendid verticality' with few decorations to obscure its form and it dominates this much redeveloped area.

Gallowgate, looking east to Belgrove Street and Abercrombie Street, c. 1910 and 2012

Gallowgate was one of the four streets of the medieval burgh of Glasgow, although nothing now remains from that period. In 1910, by which time Glasgow had developed to the west, Gallowgate was the beating heart of the east end, a proud working-class enclave, and busy enough to require a policeman on points duty. In yet another wave of redevelopment, the Victorian tenements were demolished and replaced by the social housing we see in the 2012 scene. The new units may lack the charm of the buildings they replaced, but the compensation is much improved facilities for residents.

◀ *Glasgow Green, 1900*

The present Glasgow Green has been in existence for nearly three centuries. In the eighteenth century it was used mainly for grazing, dyeing and washing but since 1857 it has been a public park serving the east end of the city. The Doulton fountain (*centre*) was designed for the Glasgow Exhibition of 1888, but was moved here in 1890. The fountain marks the golden jubilee of Queen Victoria, who looks down from the summit on four maidens. Have regard also to the forty-four-metre-high Nelson Monument (*background, centre*) of 1806 to plans by David Hamilton: the huge obelisk towers over Glasgow Green, and was the first such commemoration in Britain of Nelson's naval victories.

▲ *Glasgow Green, 2012*

Following a £4 million refurbishment programme the Doulton Fountain – the largest terracotta fountain in the world – was moved to another part of Glasgow Green, in front of the People's Palace. The McLennan Arch (*front, centre*) – once the focal point of the Adam-designed Assembly Rooms of 1792, and which were located in Ingram Street – was moved here in 1922.

St Andrew's Church, St Andrew's Square,
late nineteenth century

St Andrew's Church, St Andrew's Square, late nineteenth century and 2012

Said to be the finest church of its generation in Scotland, St Andrew's was completed in the 1750s to plans by Allan Dreghorn, a wealthy businessman and enthusiastic amateur architect. Mungo Naismith was the master mason. The design was inspired by the church of St Martin's-in-the-Field, London. Restored to former glories in 2000, the interior is sumptuous, especially the elaborate plaster work by Thomas Clayton. Note also the lines from the poetry of Robert Burns carved into the stone at the top of the front steps. St Andrew's stood in open countryside for three decades until the development began of what became St Andrew's Square. The church is now a cultural centre.

CROSS & TRONGATE, GLASGOW

◄ *Trongate from Glasgow Cross, 1903*

Trongate was named after the public weighing beam, or 'tron', and was at one time a fashionable thoroughfare along which the Tobacco Lords and other wealthy businessmen strolled. As affluent Glasgow moved west, the Trongate had by 1912 become what it is today: the people's street. This is confirmed by the number of workmen on the right of the photograph. The building with the octagonal dome (*left*) was Glasgow Cross railway station.

▲ *Trongate from Glasgow Cross, 2012*

The Tron steeple, which straddles the pavement (*left*), housed the public weighing beam and is all that remains of the original church on this site, which dates from 1492, but was destroyed in a fire of 1793. A replacement church, set back from the steeple, has been converted into the Tron theatre. The vents (*left*) ventilate the shafts of the old station.

Trongate, looking east, 1900 and 2012

Trongate in 1900 boasted many thriving businesses, some familiar in the modern age, some now long gone. The Bank of Scotland (*left, 1900*) is in the former category but Casey Ltd (*left, 1900*), which sold a complete of teeth for ten shillings or a partial set for just two shillings, is definitely one of the latter. Glasgow's penchant for tea and cakes is evident given the size and prominence of the Tron Tea Rooms (*right, 1900*). The statue of King William II, III of England, (*middle distance, 1900*) has been moved to its own garden in Cathedral Square.

St Enoch Square, early 1880s

Built between 1870 and 1876, on what had at one time been a select residential square, the St Enoch station and hotel dominated this part of the city for almost a hundred years. The hotel, with its two hundred bedrooms, was said to be the third largest in Europe. The all-male gathering pictured here might have been headed for the races, given that field glasses are being hired out (*right foreground*).

St Enoch Square, 2012

Despite fierce opposition from the public, the station and hotel were demolished in 1977 and now the St Enoch centre, a huge 1980s shopping mall, recently extended, occupies the square. At the time of construction the shopping centre was reputed to be the largest such structure in Europe, although it is one with little architectural merit. At least the quirky former underground station/travel centre dating from 1896 (*right*), a Baronial riot in sandstone, was retained.

ARGYLE ST. GLASGOW. 13,759. G.W.W.

Argyle Street, looking east, 1904 and 2012

The 1904 scene provides us with a wonderful portrait of Edwardian Glasgow. This is the city at its zenith: busy, bustling, affluent, crowded onto trams. Note the Temperance Hotel on the corner with Union Street (*left*), a feature of the time, and the vegetarian restaurant (*right*), which shows that our ancestors were more health conscious than present-day Glaswegians, given that it is now a branch of McDonalds! The most charming image is of the two little boys (*right foreground, 1904*) arm-in-arm as they cross the road.

BUCHANAN STREET GLASGOW   2991   GWW

◀ *Buchanan Street, looking south, early 1880s*

Reckoned by many good judges to be Glasgow's finest thoroughfare Buchanan Street's first manifestation was as a street of fine mansions, initiated by the eponymous Andrew Buchanan, a tobacco merchant, in the 1760s. Buchanan erected a sumptuous pile for himself and then sold further plots to his fellow businessmen, who also built large houses. By the mid nineteenth century, however, Buchanan Street was being transformed into a shopping Mecca.

▲ *Buchanan Street, looking south, 2012*

The street was pedestrianised in 1978, helping it to retain its status as the city's most upmarket shopping destination, assisted by the construction of new malls, such as Buchanan Galleries and Princes Square, and, as this photograph shows, the construction of new units continues apace. There are still many architectural gems, such as St George's Tron church (*far left, capped by obelisk*) a splendid Baroque design by William Stark, reminiscent of Hawksmoor, and completed in 1809.

29

Buchanan Street at St Vincent Place, 1912
Two of Glasgow's finest buildings, the Stock Exchange and St George's Tron, are in the centre ground. The building to the left – no. 147 Buchanan Street – is the Western Club of 1842 by David and James Hamilton, an early example of the Italianate style in Glasgow, inspired by James Hamilton's tour of the Continent. The Western was modelled on the gentlemen's clubs of London and at its peak boasted a membership of six hundred, mostly wealthy Glasgow businessmen. The Western Club has now relocated but the magnificent structure remains.

Buchanan Street at St Vincent Place, 2012

One hundred years later this is still an impressive nineteenth century townscape, although the Stock Exchange by John Burnet (1877) was covered in scaffolding when the photograph was taken. Burnet based his Gothic design for the Exchange on the Law Courts in London's Strand. Mr Craig's tearoom (*right*) is now a shop selling expensive knitwear, while the Western Club is home to the Apple Store, a twenty-first-century style icon.

◄ *Buchanan Street, looking north, 1926*

A branch of Cranston's tearooms can be seen bottom right, the eponymous Miss Kate Cranston being a pioneer of the burgeoning tearoom movement of the 1880s and 1890s. She was also a renowned patron of the arts and her premises were often used as galleries for the leading artists of the day, including the Glasgow Boys. Miss Cranston was determined to ensure that her tearooms would set new standards and in 1896 she commissioned George Walton to design the interiors of her Buchanan Street establishment, in which endeavour he was assisted by Glasgow's greatest artist and designer, Charles Rennie Mackintosh.

▲ *Buchanan Street, looking north, 2012*

The city's grandest department store, Fraser's, (*left*) comprises five nineteenth-century buildings from nos. 21–61, all of which were consumed as Fraser's expanded. Inside the grand emporium is a magnificent cast-iron saloon of 1885 with four tiers of galleries, a glazed arched roof and a highly impressive mahogany stair at the entrance. Designed by James Sellars, it is well worth a visit. The entrances for two of Glasgow's most eminent retail destinations – Argyll Arcade and Princes Square – are on the right.

Queen Street, viewed from Royal Exchange Square, 1890

The building on Ingram Street (*far left*) is the former British Linen Bank, completed in 1839 to plans by David Hamilton, who also partly designed the Royal Exchange across the road. It faces Arthur and Company's wholesale warehouse (*centre and right*), an imposing Francophile block in the elaborate style of the Second Empire. Note also the ready-for-hire 'growler' (hackney cab) in the centre foreground.

Queen Street, viewed from Royal Exchange Square, 2012
The bank building on the left was a very poor replacement for Hamilton's British Linen Bank, while the Arthur and Company warehouse had to be rebuilt in the 1940s after being hit by a Second World War bomb. At least we still have Baron Marochetti's 1844 equestrian bronze of the Duke of Wellington (*with traffic cone*!) and closer inspection of the base reveals a number of reliefs, including one depicting the Battle of Waterloo, the Iron Duke's greatest triumph.

The Royal Exchange, 1904

Royal Exchange Square is dominated by the former Royal Exchange building, which was converted by architect David Hamilton between 1827 and 1832 from the original late-eighteenth century mansion constructed by William Cunninghame. Hamilton added the huge portico with its Corinthian columns and also the cupola above. The interior – inspired by Sir John Soane's Bank of England and the Signet Library in Edinburgh – is equally impressive.

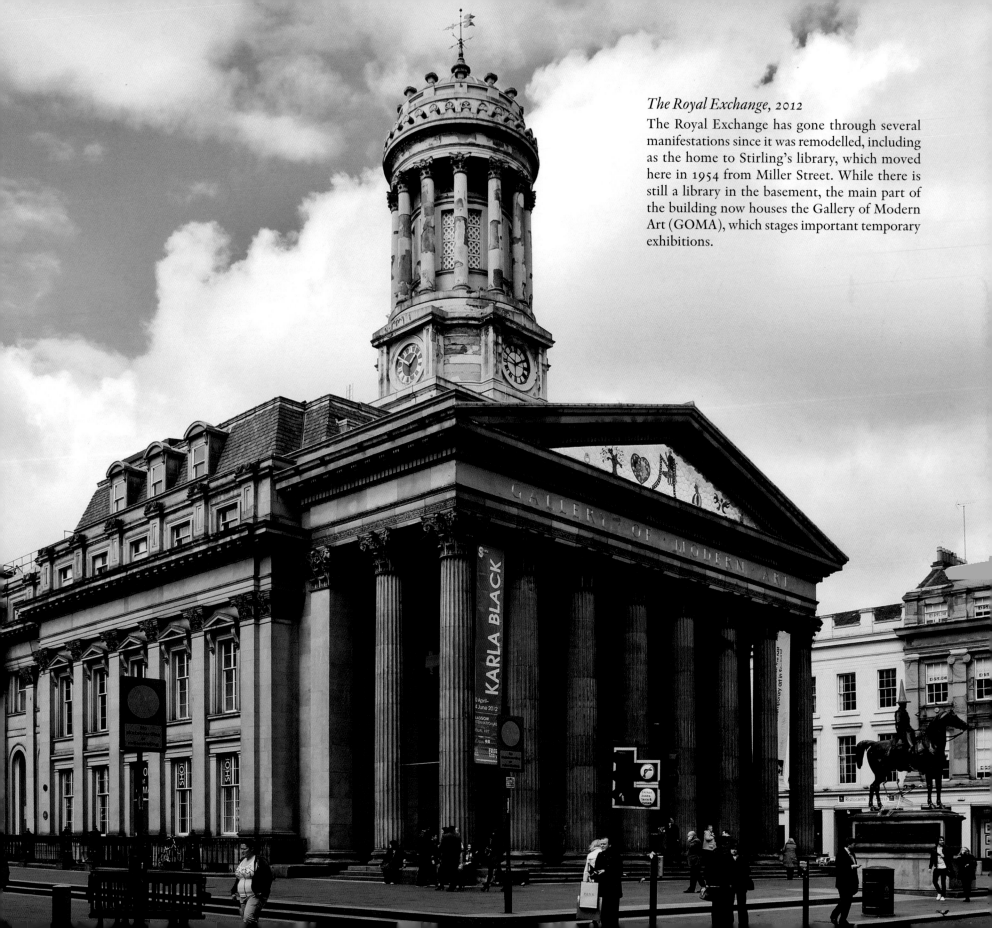

The Royal Exchange, 2012
The Royal Exchange has gone through several manifestations since it was remodelled, including as the home to Stirling's library, which moved here in 1954 from Miller Street. While there is still a library in the basement, the main part of the building now houses the Gallery of Modern Art (GOMA), which stages important temporary exhibitions.

GENERAL POST-OFFICE.   GLASGOW.

◄ *George Square and former general post office, 1904*
Completed in 1878 to plans by Robert Matheson, this dignified and beautifully proportioned Italianate structure with its intricate stonework well deserves its place in the pantheon of leading Glasgow buildings.

▲ *George Square and former general post office, 2012*
The post-office building was extended during the First World War by the addition of the two large side blocks. The statues on George Square commemorate a pair of Glasgow-born war heroes: (*left*) Field Marshal Lord Clyde (Colin Campbell), who commanded the 'thin red line' of Highlanders at the battle of Balaclava in the Crimean War; (*right*) Sir John Moore, the hero of Corunna, the Napoleonic Wars battle in which he died.

RENFIELD STREET, GLASGOW.   11,519   SVW.

Renfield Street, looking north, 1904 and 2012

The name Renfield derives from the Campbells of Blythswood, Glasgow notables of the mid seventeenth century and owners of the Blythswood estate. When the Campbells acquired a new estate in Renfrew, it was called Renfield, a name they later used for this city street. There are many fine structures in Renfield Street, although the elegant City of Glasgow Life Assurance building (*right, 1904*) has gone. Note the large present-day structure (*right, 2012*) at the top of the street, the Cineworld multiplex, from which top floors there is a magnificent view of Glasgow.

Ca' d'Oro Building, corner of Gordon Street and Union Street, 1904

Ca' d'Oro Building, corner of Gordon Street and Union Street, 2012
Both views of Union Street are dominated by the Ca' d'Oro building of 1872 (*centre and left*), which is another splendid
John Honeyman design. It was originally a furniture warehouse, while the name Ca' d'Oro comes from a restaurant
that occupied the interior from 1926. Described by one critic as a 'magnificent palazzo', Honeyman was trying to
recreate the Golden House of Venice by using contemporary materials such as cast-iron. The 2012 image shows the
Ca' d'Oro restored to its original state, with two additional bays of 1989 replacing the 1920s Art Deco extension. Note
also the magnificent Egyptian Halls (nos. 84–100), visible in the old photograph (*left*), but enveloped in a cosmetic
wall-covering in the new.

St Vincent Place, late 1890s

Leading to George Square, St Vincent Place has many distinguished commercial buildings, including J. T. Rochead's Bank of Scotland of 1869 (*background, left*), which one critic describes as 'mercantile grandeur in the form of an Italian palazzo'. It is now the Counting House pub. The former *Evening Citizen* office and printing works occupy no. 24, complete with clock. The structure that dominates the left of the photograph at nos. 30–40 was the headquarters of the Clydesdale Bank until 1902.

St Vincent Place, 2012

Next to Rochead's masterpiece, at nos. 12–16, are the former Anchor Line offices, completed in 1907 and for obvious reasons not in the photograph on the left. Two buildings on the right are worth noting: at nos. 17–29 sits the Beaux Arts Scottish Provident office and at 31–39 we have the former Scottish Amicable building. Glasgow's first fully equipped gents' public lavatory (*centre foreground in both photographs*) is still with us, although no longer operational, but, sadly, the ornate nineteenth-century lamp standard at the entrance has gone.

CENTRAL STATION, HOPE STREET, GLASGOW. 3987. G.W.W.

◀ *Central Station and the Central Hotel, from Hope Street, 1904*
The station is fronted by the Central Hotel (*centre, right*), designed by Robert Rowand Anderson, with the first phase being completed in 1884. The hotel was originally to be offices, with hotel accommodation provided across the road at 91 Hope Street. However, owners Caledonian Railways changed their minds and instructed Anderson to create a hotel that would eclipse the rival St Enoch's. Both hotel and station were extended in the early years of the twentieth century.

▲ *Central Station and the Central Hotel, from Hope Street, 2012*
The hotel was extended down Hope Street in 1908 to plans by James Miller, but the older buildings on Gordon Street (*left*) have been replaced. Hope and Gordon streets are still dominated by the huge Swedish-style clock tower of the hotel with its pyramid roof. The hotel, one of Glasgow's most iconic buildings, has recently been extensively refurbished.

Sauchiehall Street, from West Nile Street, 1890s

For much of the late nineteenth century, Sauchiehall Street was the destination of choice for the affluent consumer. Its many fashionable shops included Copland and Lye (*left, background*) which, with its four hundred shop assistants, sumptuous interiors and comprehensive range of goods, was considered one of the finest department stores in Britain. Sadly, Caledonian House – the name of the Copland and Lye building – was demolished in the 1970s to make way for the Sauchiehall Street centre.

Sauchiehall Street, from West Nile Street, 2012

Now pedestrianised, Sauchiehall Street has lost some of its lustre, although Glasgow's last traditional department store, Watt Brothers, built in two parts between 1914 and 1930 on the corner with Hope Street (*left, foreground*), is still with us. Also worthy of attention (*centre, right*) is the glorious late-Victorian facade of a former furniture warehouse, completed in 1895, now renamed the Savoy Centre.

◀ *Sauchiehall Street, looking east, 1905*
The Balmoral Hotel (*left*), a temperance establishment, is on the corner with Cambridge Street. By comparison with earlier scenes, the trams have now been electrified and no longer rely on the horse. Note also the formally dressed shoppers, perhaps another contrast with today, flocking to the fashionable shops.

▲ *Sauchiehall Street, looking east, 2012*
Dunne's department store (*left*), a stylish art deco building first used by C & A in 1929, occupies the site of the Balmoral. The fine building on the other side of Cambridge Street is, however, extant.

◀ *Empire Theatre, Sauchiehall Street, c. 1930*

The Empire Theatre was known throughout the showbiz world as the 'comic's graveyard', with one English comedian said to have fainted at the prospect of facing a Glasgow audience on a Saturday night. Designed by the renowned theatre architect, Frank Matcham, for impresario H. E. Moss, the Empire opened its doors in 1897, with seats for nearly 1,700 patrons. Closed for redevelopment in 1930 it was extended to the corner of Renfield Street, with the capacity increased to 2,100.

▲ *Empire Theatre site, Sauchiehall Street, 2012*

The final curtain for the 'comic's graveyard' was brought down in 1963, when an all-star cast gathered to bid it farewell. It was the end of a long association with theatre on this site as the Empire had itself replaced the Gaeity Theatre, which was demolished in 1896. Over the years the Matcham-designed palace of varieties played host to a veritable galaxy of stars, including Frank Sinatra, Cliff Richard and Morecambe and Wise.

Jamaica Street, looking north, 1888

When Jamaica Street was first conceived in 1761 the developers had residential property in mind. However, given its proximity to the river Clyde and Glasgow's second bridge, it quickly became a commercial hub. On the left an early department store, Walter Wilson's Grand Colosseum, is visible, complete with its own customised gas lamps.

Jamaica Street, looking north, 2012
Wilson's fine emporium is long gone. However, one of Jamaica Street's fine iron-framed warehouses (*centre, left*) has survived and is now the Crystal Palace pub/restaurant. MacSorley's, another splendid licensed premises but in red sandstone, was completed in 1897, and is notable for its etched-glass windows in the Art Nouveau style.

Theatre Royal, 1860s and Theatre Royal site, 2012, both Dunlop Street

The first theatre on this site was erected in 1782, rebuilt in 1840 and again in 1863 after a fire. The statues in the niches include Shakespeare and Garrick. In 1866 the theatre was sold to the Union Railway Company and demolished soon thereafter to make way for St Enoch station, which was itself knocked down to make way for the St Enoch shopping centre we see in the 2012 photograph. The theatre should be remembered for another reason: in 1849, sixty-five people were trampled to death after a cry of 'fire' went round the crowded auditorium. A patron overheard the manager tell an actor about a fire in another theatre and his words swept through the audience. This wholly avoidable event was one of Glasgow's worst ever tragedies and is today commemorated on a plaque next to the centre's doors.

County Buildings and Courthouses, Wilson Street, 1897
This huge Greek Revival structure – built to plans of 1841 by competition winners Clarke and Bell – occupies a whole block in the heart of Glasgow's historic Merchant City. The aim was to house the county offices, Sheriff Court and the Merchants' House under one roof. The County Buildings are particularly notable for the porticos, with their giant Classical columns, and a good example appears on the right of this photograph. The interior was equally impressive but, unfortunately, much of it was remodelled using unsuitable designs and materials.

County Buildings and Courthouses, Wilson Street, 2012
The building to the left is the David Hamilton-designed Hutchesons' Hall of 1805, built to replace Hutchesons' Hospital, which had been founded by brothers George and Thomas Hutcheson of Lambhill to care for elderly men. The brothers, noted philanthropists, also paid for Hutchesons' Grammar School, today located in the south of the city. The style, as one critic writes, is 'extremely idiosyncratic, a mixture of French Neo-classicism and the English Baroque of Wren and Gibbs, executed with some of the delicacy of Robert Adam'. Statues of the Hutchesons by James Colquhoun are visible at either end of the façade, having been moved here from the seventeenth-century hospital.

◀ *Charing Cross, c. 1901*

The Grand Hotel (*left*), designed in the French style by James Brown, opened in 1872 and was the premier establishment in the west end, described by an American visitor as 'one of the finest and best appointed hotels in Europe'. It was a victim of the redevelopment programme and the M8 motorway.

▲ *Charing Cross, 2012*

We are fortunate that the landmark Charing Cross Mansions (*centre, background*) – designed by J. J. Burnet and completed in 1891 – with its splendid tower has survived the depredations of the town planners. Described by one observer as a 'five-storey curve of rippling red stone francophilia', its French Second Empire façade curves expansively into St George's Road. Note the marvellous clock with its roman numerals and the rich carvings and sculpture that surround it. The structure on the far left, with a small clock, is the Cameron Memorial Fountain, a tribute to the eponymous Sir Charles Cameron, a Glasgow MP of the late nineteenth century.

Anderston Cross, 1900

Anderston Cross, 1900 and Anderston Cross site, 2012
In the photograph on the left, taken in 1900, a bustling community goes about its business at one of Glasgow's most important crossroads. However, like many other important Glasgow landmarks Anderston Cross was swept away in the 1960s, in this instance to make way for the M8 motorway. About the only thing the two scenes have in common is that both feature railway stations. It is now hard to imagine that Anderston was once a thriving independent burgh on the edge of Glasgow, with its own town council and civic institutions.

ST GEORGE'S CROSS, GLASGOW. 43086. J.V.

St George's Cross, c. 1900 and 2012

Clarendon Place (*centre, both photographs*) with its fine portico dates from the late 1830s and was to have been part of a grand circus. The aim of the developers was to form an imposing gateway out of the city, but in the event only Clarendon Place went ahead. The tram in the older image is headed for Maryhill barracks, now demolished. Thanks to the incursions of the M8 motorway little else has survived of the Victorian townscape, although St Mary's cathedral and Lansdowne church can be seen in the distance on Great Western Road.

Park Parish Church, Park Circus Place, 1868

The splendid Park church was completed in 1868 to plans by J. T. Rochead. It is, according to one writer, 'a striking adaptation of West of England Perpendicular'. The fine Italianate building to the left, which is in Lynedoch Street, is the former Trinity College, designed by Charles Wilson, which, with its three towers, dominates the skyline. Once a theological institution, and then part of Glasgow University, the building has been converted into flats.

Park Parish Church, Park Circus Place, 2012

Despite a considerable public outcry, Rochead's Park church was demolished in 1968 to make way for a dreary reinforced concrete office block, leaving only its tall, distinguished tower still standing. Charles Wilson was not only responsible for Trinity College but was also the architect and planner we must thank for the fine residential terraces of the Park, or Woodlands Hill, as this area is known. Indeed some commentators take the view that Wilson's townscape is the finest example of Victorian town planning in Britain.

◀ *Great Western Road, looking east, 1905*
A wonderful vista of one of the city's most fashionable streets, with some outstanding buildings. Great Western Bridge (*middle, left and right*), of 1891, has been described as 'a classic of late Victorian engineering'. Because it is level with the roadway at both ends, the bridge can easily be overlooked when a crossing is made, but it is highly impressive when viewed from the riverside. Note also the sign for Kelvinbridge underground station (*right, background*).

▲ *Great Western Road, looking east, 2012*
The church closest to the camera is Lansdowne parish church of 1863, designed by John Honeyman, one of Scotland's leading ecclesiastical architects. With its slender and graceful spire, 218-foot high, it is considered by many to be the finest Victorian Gothic church in Scotland. Further down Great Western Road sits St Mary's Episcopal cathedral, designed by Sir George Gilbert Scott.

Great Western Road, looking west, 1905

Great Western Road, looking west, 2012
The entrance to the Botanic Gardens is on the right (*both photographs*), at the corner of Great Western Road and Queen Margaret Drive. The interesting building to the left in the 1905 image, with the golden onion-shaped domes, is, as the sign (*visible with magnifying glass*) indicates, the Botanic Gardens station of the Caledonian Railway. This delightful confection, designed by James Miller and operational from the 1890s, ceased to function as a station in the 1950s and was destroyed by fire in 1970.

Botanic Gardens, 1897

Botanic Gardens, 2012

As a perusal of both then-and-now photographs confirms, little appears to have changed down the years in one of Glasgow's best-loved spots. The Botanic Gardens were originally situated at the west side of Sauchiehall Street but, in a quest for purer air, were relocated to their present location in Great Western Road in 1842. The highlight of the Botanics, as the gardens are invariably called, is the giant Kibble Palace (*right*), a dramatic glass conservatory shaped rather like a mushroom, which was donated to the council by John Kibble in 1871, having been originally destined for his mansion at Loch Long. The building to the left is the Palm House.

KELVINGROVE MUSEUM. WEST END PARK. GLASGOW. 1343. G.W.W.

Kelvingrove House, Kelvingrove Park, 1877

Kelvingrove House was an important classical mansion, built for Lord Provost Patrick Colquhoun, a wealthy merchant as well as a politician. It was completed in 1792, probably to a design by Robert Adam, who was arguably Scotland's most eminent architect and the driving force behind the eighteenth century Classical revival on both sides of the border. After the house was bought by the council, it became Glasgow's first museum and art gallery and was extended by the addition of a new block with Classical columns (*left*).

Kelvingrove House site, Kelvingrove Park, 2012
Kelvingrove House was demolished to make way for the Glasgow International Exhibition of 1901. Its exact location has been confirmed by reference to an old Ordnance Survey map, which shows that Colquhoun's mansion stood on ground now occupied by this very colourful roller-skating arena, flanked by playgrounds, in the south section of the park. Kelvingrove House's cultural functions were taken over by Kelvingrove art gallery, visible in the background.

FOUNTAIN AND UNIVERSITY. WEST END PARK. GLASGOW. 1340. G.W.W.

◀ *Stewart Memorial Fountain, Kelvingrove Park, mid-to-late 1880s*

The Stewart Memorial Fountain was erected by Glasgow's water commissioners in 1872 to commemorate Lord Provost Robert Stewart of Murdostoun, who was a leading light in the development of the city's water supply. An architectural competition attracted fifty entries and the winner was James Sellars, a then unknown architect, with his French Gothic extravaganza. With its splendid gargoyles, lions, unicorns and fish – by local sculptors John Mossman and James Young – the finished product was rightly admired by critics and public alike.

▲ *Stewart Memorial Fountain, Kelvingrove Park, 2012*

The main theme of the Stewart Fountain is Sir Walter Scott's narrative poem *Lady of the Lake*, set in the Trossachs, the area in which the main source of Glasgow's water, Loch Katrine, is situated. Note in particular the seven-foot statue of Ellen Douglas (the 'Lady of the Lake') on top of the central cluster – and also the bronze of Robert Stewart at a lower level. In the background, we can see that Glasgow University's iconic tower now has its spire in place.

Glasgow University from Kelvingrove Park, 1904

The decision in the 1860s to move Glasgow University (*right*) from High Street to its current home in Gilmorehill was a controversial one. The old university consisted of some of the finest seventeenth century buildings in Scotland and many felt they should have been restored. However, the university accepted an offer from a railway company to buy the High Street site and then commissioned George Gilbert Scott (the English architect behind the Foreign Office in London) to create a new seat of learning. Despite fierce criticism from Glasgow's architectural establishment his Gothic Revival design, with its 100-foot tower and spire, is certainly striking.

Glasgow University from Kelvingrove Park, 2012
The bowling green (*foreground*) is still in existence today, although when this photograph was taken it was being refurbished for the Commonwealth Games, to be held in Glasgow in 2014. The imposing building to the left is Kelvingrove art gallery.

◀ *Kelvingrove Art Gallery and Museum, from below Park Terrace, 1904*
This red-sandstone extravaganza is quite simply one of the most striking buildings in Scotland. Paid for by a combination of the profits from the Glasgow International Exhibition of 1888, public subscription and funds from Glasgow Corporation it was completed in 1901 to plans by Sir J. W. Simpson and E. J. Milner Allen, who won the brief after yet another controversial architectural competition. The style, according to one writer, is Hispanic Baroque, and the exterior is embellished by fine sculptures and carvings.

▲ *Kelvingrove Art Gallery and Museum, from below Park Terrace, 2012*
Kelvingrove, visible above the trees, was restored to former glories after a £35-million refurbishment in 2006. It has an impressive collection of sculpture, jewellery, ceramics and natural-history pieces. Most importantly it houses probably the finest civic art collection in Britain, including works by Rembrandt, Monet, Picasso and Dali. Both the Western Infirmary (*right*) and Yorkhill Hospital (*left*) can be seen in the background.

The Western Infirmary, Glasgow. 2826. G.W.W.

Western Infirmary, 1904

Western Infirmary, 2012

When Glasgow University moved to Gilmorehill, it was inevitable that a new hospital would be required to link into the medical faculty. The result was the Western Infirmary (*opposite page*). The huge Scots Baronial edifice (1874) was built to plans by John Burnet senior, and later added to as the hospital expanded. The centre turrets were inspired by the gables of Glamis Castle. Little remains of the original hospital, which is now dominated by the eleven-storey main block of the 1970s. In the left foreground (*this page*) we have the Cameronians (Scottish Rifles) war memorial, a highly evocative tribute to the fallen of two world wars.

Glasgow Bridge, looking south, 1914

Sometimes known as Jamaica Bridge, in 1899 it replaced a fine seven-arched structure by Thomas Telford dating from 1835, which was judged too narrow for shipping and traffic. The bridge would have been even wider and taller but there was much public opposition to losing the outline of the great engineer's masterpiece, as well as concern about the cost of a larger structure. In the end, therefore, the replacement was almost identical to Telford's original design.

Glasgow Bridge, looking south, 2012

While Glasgow Bridge was once the main transpontine link to Jamaica Street from south of the Clyde it has been usurped by the mammoth Kingston Bridge, completed in 1970. This no doubt accounts for the disparity in traffic flows compared to 1914.

ANNAN. 6424.

River Clyde, from Govan, 1905 and 2012
At the time the photograph on the preceding page was taken, Glasgow was the workshop of the world. The busy river Clyde – with its slipways, docks, chimneys and merchant ships – clearly shows just how important the city was. Today the Clyde may not be the vital commercial artery it once was but there is still much to admire, not least the striking Riverside Museum, which houses Glasgow's fine collection of transport artefacts. The tall ship, the *Glenlee* of 1896, moored next to the museum, is also open to visitors.

EMBARKING AT THE BROOMIELAW, GLASGOW. 5066. G.W.W.

The Broomielaw, 1904
Edwardian Glasgow loved its trips 'doon the watter' to places like Dunoon, Rothesay, Millport and Largs, as this evocative photograph, ferries bursting with passengers, shows. We may never know the precise functions of the buildings that line Broomielaw, most of which have been demolished, but they certainly look interesting.

The Broomielaw, 2012

This section of the Clyde is now known as Atlantic Quay. The former Clyde Port Authority, with dome, is on the far right. Considered one of Glasgow's most impressive buildings, both internally and externally, and designed by J. J. Burnet, it dates from 1886 but was later extended in 1908. The magnificent statuary and carvings, which include Neptune and seahorses, as well as several prominent Scots, should not be missed. In its heyday, the Port Authority – or Clyde Navigation Trust as it then was – rivalled even the city council in power and influence and its place of business reflects that status.

St Andrew's Cross, 1917 and 2012

Pollokshaws Road meets Eglinton Street at Eglinton Toll – at one time called St Andrew's Cross, as the name on the front of the distinctive tenement block (*centre, both photographs*) indicates. St Andrew's electricity works, completed in 1900, (*right, both photographs*) has lost the giant twin cooling towers and like Eglinton Toll itself is a shadow of its former self. Sadly, the fine shelter, to the right of the tram bound for Langside in the 1917 scene, has also gone.

Caledonia Road church, 1910

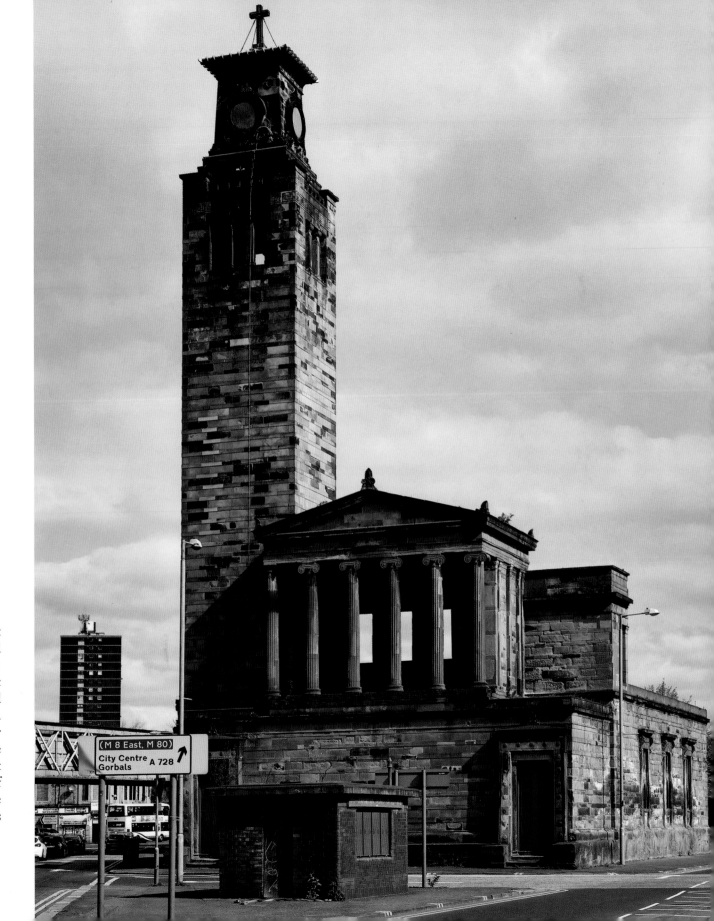

Caledonia Road church, 2012

Dating from the 1850s this was the first church designed by the man considered by many to be Glasgow's finest architect: Alexander 'Greek' Thomson. An eclectic Classical mix of Italianate tower and Greek Ionic temple, underpinned by a tall plinth, it is a pleasant surprise for motorists driving north through the Gorbals, despite the serious damage it suffered after a 1965 fire. Badly in need of refurbishment – several schemes have been mooted, but to no avail – Thomson's masterpiece awaits a saviour.

VIEW FROM THE FLAGSTAFF. SOUTH SIDE PARK, GLASGOW. 1295. G.W.W.

Queen's Park, view from the flagstaff, 1877

Queen's Park, view from the flagstaff, 2012

Queen's Park Baptist church (*left*) was in the process of construction when the old photograph was taken and had not yet acquired its spire. While the 1877 vista is that of a city in the throes of an industrial boom, with the huge smoke-billowing chimneys, the 2012 equivalent portrays a more pleasant environment, so much so that the Campsie Hills are visible in the distance.

Acknowledgements

First published in 2012 by Fort Publishing Ltd,
Old Belmont House, 12 Robsland Avenue, Ayr, KA7 2RW

'Then' photographs courtesy of:

University of Aberdeen, George Washington Wilson collection:
Front cover, title page, pages 24, 26, 28, 34, 38, 40, 42, 44, 46, 48, 54, 74, 76, 82, 88, 94

Annan Galleries: Pages 4, 12, 14, 16, 22, 32, 36, 50, 60, 62, 68, 70, 78, 80, 86

Mitchell Library, Glasgow:
Pages 6, 66, 92

Francis Frith Collection @ http://francisfrith.com
Pages 58, 72

University of Glasgow library:
Page 18

Newsquest (*Herald and Evening Times*)
Page 52

Burrell Gallery, Glasgow
Page 64

All 2012 photographs by Duncan I. McEwan

Contact from copyright holders welcome

Graphic design of cover by Mark Blackadder

Front-cover titles by Doreen Shaw

Typeset by 3btype.com

Printed in China by Imago Ltd

ISBN: 978-1-905769-38-4